GUT REACTION

Elaine Randell

NORTH AND SOUTH

Twickenham and Wakefield

Acknowledgements: thanks are given to the Editors of Rock Drill and to Pig Press.

Book design by Peterjon Skelt

Published by North and South at
23 Egerton Road, Twickenham, Middlesex TW2 7SL and at
77 Lincoln Street, Wakefield, West Yorkshire WF2 0ED.
The signed edition is of 26 copies lettered A-Z and signed by the author.

Typeset by
Wordsmiths Ltd, 55 East Road, London N1 6AH.
Printed by
K & N Press Ltd, Molesey Avenue, West Molesey, Surrey KT8 0RY.

British Library Cataloguing in Publication Data

Randell, Elaine

Gut Reaction.
I. Title
823'.914 [F] PR6068.A56

ISBN 1 870314 02 6
ISBN 1 870314 03 4 Signed Edition

North and South is a member of the Association of Little Presses

This book is dedicated to all those who work in the caring professions; who seek to improve the quality of others' lives.

I shall not weary you with poems,
With unfading memory, the earth
Shall be made over; this is our corner,
Where this hope is.

Ponies stand head to head,
Sharing their breath in the frosty air.

Even at mid-day,
The mist does not clear, the night
Will be long: it is ten
Past twelve, there is nothing

To fear, we shall live after
This day, this day.

John Riley
1937-1948

CONTENTS

Introduction

This collection of prose pieces began in 1977 and spans ten years. It represents part of my daily life as a social worker in child care and mental health matters. The pieces come from direct work with the individuals concerned.

Without exception all the people and incidents are true but any identifying attributes have been changed to maintain confidentiality.

The humour, courage, conflict and pain contained in the lives described is clear. The reader may be disturbed by the realities of the facts.

I thank all those concerned for allowing me to listen.

Elaine Randell
Kent, August 1987

Him on foam and me on fibreglass

"You see the thing was that at the time he was on Foam and I was on Fibreglass so I had to keep bumping into him didn't I? Even after I'd run over him that Sunday I'd go to work at the factory and there he'd be on Foam and I'd be right next to him on Fibreglass. Actually that Sunday had started off quite well all things considered. He offered to take our old table over to Sheila's in the back of the car and I drove. I felt good, in reasonable spirits I'd say. I wasn't especially cross with him or anything, no more than usual seeing how he was always an aggravating bugger at the best of times. But anyway, I offered to drive and he agreed, he always agreed about everything. Well, on the way over we started talking about Sheila, she's my daughter by my first marriage and he began making comments about how pretty she was. I didn't say a thing. When we got there with the tools, he opened the back of the car, took the table out and stood there in the middle of the drive looking at me in that way of his, you know, sort of sly as though he hated me and I looked at him, and he looked back at me. I thought to myself 'I really wish you were dead, that you just didn't exist anymore'. Before I knew where I was I'd run over him, twice in fact. But he wasn't hurt, hardly at all. I was surprised - but then he always had a hard head. When you think about it it's awful. I had four children by him and still I'd felt nothing but for the fact that I wished he didn't exist.

"Of course now he is living with Sheila, his own stepdaughter, it's disgusting.

"But as I say it's worse at work because I see him. What with him on Foam and me on Fibreglass."

To always look after it

A Monday. I go and see Richard at the children's home. I'm told that over the weekend Richard committed another offence with some of his friends and that he will be interviewed again by the Police today. Richard took some beer from the backyard of a shop with a girl a year older than himself. At sixteen she had already served her time in a girls' Borstal. Between them they climbed over the fence, took six cans of drink and a bottle of sherry. They came home after drinking the beer with red faces and pockets bulging. It is the girl's eighteenth offence and Richard's third.

I wait for Richard to return from school so I can talk with him about the events. Eventually he shows up. I watch him get off the school bus outside the children's home. He is laughing, his brand new outsized school blazer is stiff and boxlike. He looks up at the window and seeing me he makes a face and laughs. I ask him about his weekend. He tells me that the day before the offences occurred he went home to see his parents. In the morning his mother took him to the park, handed him her wedding ring and said for him to always look after it as she had taken many sleeping pills that morning, and that she was going to die. He ran and found a Policeman and within an hour his mother was hospitalised again and Richard was taken back to the children's home.

"Tell me Richard about the shop you broke into and the beer and sherry."

"What beer?" he says. I tell him he knows what beer. "Oh, that beer - anyway I was sick."

For me to clear up

I am called out as an emergency to visit the family home of a woman in her late fifties who tried to take her own life last week by swallowing every pill she could find in the house. The house is a council property with no garden. It overlooks a bald brown playing area where the unwanted dogs meet up, fight, make their mess, make other dogs and frighten the children. Inside, the home is tidy and very clean. The woman cries as soon as I ask how she is. "My husband is dead," she says, "he was crawling around on all fours at night with the pain of it. I'm glad he's out of that. He used to try and reach the bathroom, he didn't want to make a mess for me to clear up, you see." Yes, I did see. I could see from her anxious wringing hands and her lined brow and her thin, shapeless body. "He died so suddenly and then within a few months our daughter, Frances, told me she was pregnant, sixteen years old. The baby was born eight months later, little Sam, beautiful baby. I brought him here, she went to work. I found it hard to manage on a widow's benefit but I got free coal from the Pit and mates of Stan's visited regularly and gave me a few bob now and then. I loved little Sammy. She just upped and went you see, taking Sammy with her. No warning. He was my life, my grandson." I watch her constantly wringing hands and her feet moving around in the oversized slippers. "When Frances met this lad they were going to get married. I was pleased for her, he seemed a nice boy. She wanted a white wedding and a reception from here. I agree to do all the catering for them and so for weeks I prepared food for the big day. Bearing in mind I'd just recovered from her dad dying I did well to work so hard. I paid for it all out of my cleaning job. It was all laid out on the front room tables, I borrowed glasses and chairs and cutlery from half the people up the street. I came down from bed at 7.00am to find Frances and Sammy already up and dressed and her looking sheepish holding a note. 'What's happening here?' I said.

"'I didn't think I'd see you, mum,' she said, 'I was going to leave this note.' She handed it to me and then went out the back door with Sammy. Before I realised what was happening a taxi had taken them off. I read the note, it said that she was sorry, very sorry about it, her and Joe were already married, they'd done it last week in a Registry Office with strangers as witnesses. The big white wedding was off, he couldn't go through with it. The reception was off too. She'd decided to go to London to live with his parents and Sammy. She said she didn't know when she'd be round again. I haven't seen them since. I had all the food laid out, can you imagine it? I couldn't take it all in what with her dad dying like that and all of it. That's why I took all those pills. I am alone."

Outside on the bald playing field the dogs yap and chase. The woman sitting inside by the fire roaring away all the free coalboard fuel, next to her photo of herself and her husband, a wartime shot with him upright and handsome, his arms round her and both of them laughing.

As much as it takes

A short man, Mick, aged thirty nine is 'balding too fast for comfort' he tells me. His large deep set eyes poke out of a ruby red face that bulges over the dark moustache that he grew last year 'in attempt to make my face seem more interesting'. He has a rash over one cheek and ulcers in his mouth which all add to the general feelings of complaint and disfigurement of which he speaks. He talks with one eye on the clock every so often and the other on his wrist-watch. I ask if he is in a hurry. "I've got no plans, there's no rush, no-one at home waiting for me. That's just it you see, when I was at work I used to race home to see the kids before they went to bed, try and play with them as much as possible. They do love me those kids you know. I brought them up when they were babies. Sandra had that postnatal depression or whatever it's called, she couldn't or wouldn't do a thing for months. When those kids screamed in the night it was me that got up and saw to them, still would now if I had the chance. I'll give as much as it takes to get those kids back again. No-one's going to tell me that my own kid don't want to see me. I can understand Sharon saying what she did and anyway I know that Sandra's been poisoning her with stories about me but Lenny, I just will not accept that my little Lenny doesn't want to see his daddy again. Lenny is only seven for godsake and Sandra sits there telling me that he even refuses to speak to me on the 'phone. It's nearly a year since I've seen them now. I have tried, really tried. OK, so I have been working out in Saudi for nine months but it was only to raise a home and money for those kids. You don't seem to understand that Sandra's not a real mother, she can't look after those kids properly, she can't even look after herself, look at the state of her. I admit that Sharon is different, she's always been a quiet kid. My nerves were bad when we had her as a baby, I was worried about debts. But Lenny, my little Lenny he must want to go Drag Racing with his daddy again, he must. I'm going to give as much as it takes to see those kids again. Whatever's gone on with Sandra and me is water under the bridge now, why she can't see that I don't know. We did have some rows I admit. There was a lot of shouting but it wasn't only me they saw fighting. Sandra can land a blow or two I can tell you, she's a strong girl. Once she slashed my arm with a razor". He lifts his shirt sleeve to show me the scar with stretches from above the elbow to his wrist. "OK, so I forgot Lenny's birthday once or twice but I was busy, I've had worries. l love that kid. I think about him all the time. I never go past a shop without wondering if Lenny would like this or that. Lenny is a daddy's boy, always has been always will be. He'll come round in the end. Whatever it takes I'm going to make that kid see sense. I am his dad after all. Nothing can change that can it?"

"No," I say, "Nothing can change that".

Gerry

I'm talking to Rita in the hospital. She has put on weight and her new skirt rides up over her knees as we sit on the plastic cumfy chairs in the Dayroom. Rita has always liked to look nice and today she shows me her new jumper and skirt recently bought from a catalogue. Round her neck Rita wears a tiny gold heart that she tells everyone her husband has bought for her, but Rita and I both know that she herself bought it last year, as her husband Gerry has been in prison now for six.

"Some of the things that my Gerry used to get me to do for him before he went inside, really when I think about it I could scream, no wonder I've had this breakdown. I remember the night he took me out on a job with him because his mate Brian wouldn't come. I had to stand outside in a yard and hold a ladder while he climbed up really high and got into the top attic windows so he could drop down into the stairwell and then into the shop without starting the burglar alarm off. I will say this for Gerry, he was very good at it, that as well. We got through thousands of pounds together before he got caught. But I was telling you. Gerry told me to wear something dark for this job so I couldn't be seen easily, so I wore my plunge neckline black dress with the slit up the side, black tights and my black boots. So I'm standing there in the freezing cold like this holding the ladder while Gerry gets up there. Once he's up top I'm supposed to wait half an hour while he gets the gear together and comes down before we shoot off. Anyway I'm standing there at the ladder bloody freezing to death when this bloke walks up to me and says 'Hello Gorgeous where are you going?' What could I say, I couldn't tell him could I? So I wink at him and he gets in the back of the car. He gave me £5. Well, by the time he's finished and trying to make another ate with me for next week Gerry's up the ladder shouting 'Rita, Rita, where are you' and I go off running across the yard. We got away alright but when we get home he says to me 'You alright Gal?' I tell him that I'm fine. 'Only you look a bit flushed I'd say'. It's just the night air I tell him. If he found out he'd kick the bloke's head in. He was like that was Gerry."

You can't odds what your eyes have seen

"We come round the back that afternoon and made a cut through the cul-de-sac when Darren pipes up 'Here that's dad's lorry'. I was amazed but then you can't odds what your eyes have seen can you? I told him it was just parked there because dad's mate had borrowed it but inside I was afraid. I knew something was up. Anyway we passed by on the other side with my yanking Darren not to gape like that and got him home as smart as possible.

"When his dad got home late I asked him if he's had a good day. 'Tiring pet,' he said, 'Tiring'. I said nothing.

"A few days later I picked Darren up from school and on the way home he pipes up again. 'I saw dad today with a bird and she hasn't arf got big tits.' I kept on walking and into the front room where he sat snoring. 'Hello love' I said kissing him on the cheek. He just carried on snoring, must have been worn out. I went upstairs and wrapped all his dirty washing into a big towel and put it all into a plastic Tesco bag. I took it downstairs and woke him up with a shake. 'Trevor,' I called, 'Sweet Trevor, you know your mate what's round the corner, the one that wears the skirt, well this is a present from me to her.' Then I whacked him hard across the head with the bundle and told him to go. He went.

"But our Darren's so rebellious now. I reckon he might be better off without me. He's that mouthy. He's always on about his dad, how we've never seen him since that day. He often asks me whether it was his fault, if he hadn't seen the lorry that day you see he thinks I wouldn't have found out and his dad would be here still.

"I always tell him 'You can't odds what your eyes have seen, chuck' and then I give him a cuddle but he shrugs it off. He doesn't arf look like his dad."

Making progress

"I would have written sooner, the letter said, but he seemed to be making such good progress. He was eating very well to the last - everything mashed up finely as he liked it. His sleeping wasn't as sound as usual, but then with him being unwell we had to strap him down that much firmer to make sure he wasn't going to fall out.

"Always a smile though, everyday he smiled at us - our golden boy we called him.

"I'm sorry to break this news to you in a letter but we tried to get you on the phone and the social worker called round several times and was told you were in Spain on holiday. I know it's a few years since you saw him but he really came on well in the last two years especially. The illness wasn't very serious at first, the doctor gave him some antibiotics and drained his tubes. You know how often these childreen need such special care.

"We all thought he'd rally round as he was doing so well and playing his little card games on his own as usual. The doctor said he didn't suffer at all at the end, just slipped away into a deep sleep. Matron has his belongings here for you to collect when you want to, there's not much just his toys and a few clothes and his photos of you the family at home.

"Yes, I'm sorry to break this news to you in a letter and as I say, I would have written sooner to say he was ill but he was making such good progress..."

That sort of man

"Fourteen months ago he had stroke and died. Just like that. No warning. They wore him out one way and another. All that work to do and they never thought he might want a day off. I'd never been on holiday myself and neither had he, well it isn't easy with stock work. You just can't leave animals and they never offered to help out. One morning he said to me 'Dot, they're trying to kill me before I retire, trying to get the last drop out of me before I go.' Of course when he did drop dead they didn't like it when I said that he been worked too hard, they didn't like that at all, said it was his fault if he didn't speak up a bit. Two years ago he was up every night with the lambing, making money for them. I never see a sheep now without wondering about him and if he'd delivered that ewe. Then it doesn't do to go on thinking about it, dwelling on it. I just feel half dead myself you see. You can't be married for thirty odd years and not feel it can you? But then he didn't suffer at the end, he wasn't that sort of man to drag anything on, not even death. I can't beleive that I'll spend the rest of my life without seeing him. I always imagine he'll walk back in through the door like he always did saying 'Cup of tea Dot will do well'. I look outside and think he's only round the back, he'll be in soon, but then it hits me and I think - he's not at the farm, he's dead."

We walk through the cottage hallway into the other room and on the hallstand are all his old coats waiting for him. He was a huge man and the coats are as big as blankets. Sheep wool and string hang from the pockets.

"I can't start life again although people tell me I must. My friends take me to the Zodiac Club, we do laugh I'll say that. I've never drunk before but it seems all the women do now. We never went out you see. I worked at the house cleaning and he was the Stockman, that's how we met. Never regret a single day of it: ... but they shouldn't have overworked him, they should have helped him slow up. Lambing, lambing, lambing, calving, calving, calving - all for the money in their pockets. Now I have to leave here as I'm no use to them. I have to find another home. A man from the council came and offered me a flat but I can't live in a flat in town, I'm too used to fields and the lane here. I keep on at the boy to get a farm job like his father but he wants a factory job. Well you can't blame him really can you, having seen what it did to his dad in the end.

"Well I must say though, my husband loved it here. Watching the rain come down from his little hut out on the marsh. He loved that little hut. I can't bring myself to go out there. But I will, before we go. I must. We were going to go on holiday together when he retired. My daughter's asked me to go to Butlins. I'm going. My first ever holiday. I suppose if he'd come with us then he would only have spent half his time wondering what the animals were doing and worry and all. He was that sort of man you see."

Family

"When my brother Carl was six we were evicted from Castle Street. I remember it distinctly because it was his birthday and the woman next door had made him a cake that he was clutching when the bailiffs came and he was flung by my mother across my small shoulders to stop him crying. Instead he yelled louder and was promptly very sick as he had also, that very morning, sunk his teeth into my father's tobacco and swallowed enough for a good smoke. In fact my father was more intent on shouting to my brother 'That'll bloody teach you to go poking!' then he was talking to the bailiff when they marched through our hall. We went that day to live with my Uncle

Ernest who ran a grocery shop the other side of town. It was a fine greengrocery and my Uncle's pride and joy. His wife, my Aunt Cissie, was none too pleased at the prospect of us four invading her neat and tidy home but Uncle Ernest had said 'You can't see your own brother and his kids out on the street can you?' and that was that, we were in; at least for four months. That was the limit according to Aunt Cissie. My father said it would be just a for a few weeks until work was found and that all that was needed was a place for the wife and kids to lay their heads as my brother and I would be at school and he and my mother would be out at work.

"The only thing my parents did well was to argue. They fought over everything possible to discuss or not discuss. Nothing was too slight to argue about. Never was there a day I can recall when my mother wasn't in tears or silent. My father was constantly smoking and his nicotine stained fingers were a constant source of mystery to me. Over the four months exactly that we lived with Aunt Cissie and Uncle Ernest not a day went by without Aunt Cissie reminding us of how much longer we had left to stay. 'Two months and sixteen days and mind you don't steal any apples or grapes from the shop and clean that sink.' By constrast Uncle Ernest was quite a wag. Carl and I adored him and could never control our giggles when we saw him mimic Aunt Cissie from behind crates of fruit that were always piled up the shop.

"At six years old Carl would run through the shop yelling and clutched at everything in his passage in order to place it straight away in his mouth before anyone could see. Often it was a potato and sometimes the bright yellow moon-like grapefruits would catch his eye and in it would go. Sooner or later chunks of all sorts met up with the bits of tocacco, hairgrips, coal and paper that lurked inside him. My mother always said it was because she'd breast fed him for too long. My father said it was because he was loopy.

"My mother's nerves became terribly bad after the eviction and she spent most of her time on her work-free days tidying up after us or keeping us quiet and unpicking the sleeve of her home knitted cardigan. Eventually she had only one sleeve intact and an enormous ball of olive green wool. My mother worked in the laundry a mile or so away and the continual steam in which she worked made her hair fall in minute ringlets around her head as though it were on fire.

"Looking back I suppose my mother was a very attractive woman and given all the continual rush and stress of her whole life it is amazing how she looked as good as she did. My father was a very stocky man who was balding fast. He was always quite well turned out in spite of our financial setup and he usually wore a three piece suit which although had seen better days he always had it cleaned and pressed by my Mother at the laundry every other week.

"Eventually my father found work. It was in a bookbindery in the centre of town. He was no craftsman himself but he processed the accounts and new orders which in those days were plentiful. He had so many changes of job throughout my short lifetime, which by now was ten years, and considering how difficult work was to come by it was a small miracle that he was rarely unemployed. However all this hard work never seemed to get us anywhere and we were always in dreadful debt. He drank heavily and although I never saw him unconscious he was either very merry or extremely nasty. He virtually chained smoked much to my mother's horror and spent at least a quarter of his waking life in the betting shop; hence our eviction from Castle Steet and arrival of the bailiff.

"Uncle Ernest and my father had been raised in the North part of London that is now fashionable. They were two of eight brothers only three of whom now survived, the others having died in childhood and the last one alongside of my grandmother, who being undernourished and doubtless exhausted shuffled off this mortal coil at the delivery and prospect of her eighth child. Father and Uncle were then raised partially in an orphanage from the ages of six and seven respectively. Their father was killed in the first world war, no one knew where exactly but it was suspected to be in Southern France. They therefore had a scanty memory of their parents and I frequently asked them both for stories of their childhood which I found fascinating and rather daunting. Neither could understand my interest in the past or them as children bearing in mind that they were always telling me off for being one myself.

"Carl and I enjoyed living in the greengrocers for it was a brand new experience and playground for us. We found sources of entertainment in the earth the potatoes arrived in and gazed at the exotic pictures on the sides of the boxes in which the imported fruit was packed. There were lemons from Cyprus, oranges from Spain, bananas from the Canaries and swedes from Devon. These magnificent dusky red objects were never quite the same for me after I stood next to Uncle Ernest as he unpacked a particularly ripe smelling box to discover the carcase of a dead sheep inside. The beetroots would be boiled in the yard in an old zinc bath and the pink dye ran all over the lawn much to Carl's delight. Uncle Ernest hosed the area down once a week and somehow or another Carl would end up with his clothes soaked and face beetroot red.

"Aunt Cissie and my mother got on together in a passing sort of a way. They both sympathised with the other for being married to a Clark which was my family name. They had in fact done some of their courting together when they were young having met the brothers at the same place on the same day. This, I understand, was during my Aunt Cissie's period of employment in a florist's shop in the centre of Pimlico and my father and Uncle had gone together into the West End in search of a job. They had stopped at the florist shop to enquire directions to a local factory. Indeed it was my Father who invited out Aunt Cissie and to make up a foursome she suggested she bring with her a neighbour's best friend's daughter who was staying at the time and needs 'a bit of a shake up'. The courtship, it seems, progressed quickly from there but halfway through they changed partners and my father ended up proposing to my mother in a matter of six weeks. A year later Ernest had married Cissie and by that time I was born and I am therefore present in all their wedding photographs as a tiny baby wrapped in a shawl in mother's arms. The florist's shop was owned by Aunt Cissie's parents. They also owned two greengrocery businesses which were in South London. They presented these to the couple on their marriage. They were a childless couple, a factor that had caused Cissie great periods of sadness throughout their married life and one that she now got over by claiming that she loathed small children due to the amount of mess and chaos that accompanied them. Ernest and Cissie were a devoted couple in their own way, so very different from my parents' constant battling. Cissie shouted a lot and nagged openly but she was tender in her off-guarded moments and certainly Uncle Ernest praised his wife's management abilities and had deep respect of her despite his often tormenting jokes practical and otherwise. Having us come to live with them over this period obviously brought their lives into a different focus and little Carl benefitted from all the extra attention he received from his Uncle which he never or rarely received from my father. My mother, being as harrassed as she was, had little time ever to talk to us boys and I found myself arranging my own care and devices much of the time. Largely it meant keeping out of my father's way, unless of course he'd had a win at the bookies, in which case he would pick me up on his knee and say 'Come here little one, take that frown off your face, here's a bob or two for some sweets'. So I would learn to take advantage of these times and seek pleasure with my father when I could."

When he kicked her

Mrs W comes into the office to see me. Three years ago she placed her two children into care because she 'couldn't love them or stand their constant arguing'. Mrs W visits the children every month; they are usually pleased to see her but recently their interest in her has begun to wane. Mrs W is crying as she sits down and she doesn't stop. She has one eye the other having been removed by her own father's boot when he kicked her as a small child. Mrs W is married to a man half her age and size who injures her too but she rarely leaves him for longer than a day or two. "I'm upset because my mum called me a slut. This bloke see he bought me a cup of tea in the Transport Cafe when I was running from Bob the night he assaulted me. Everything is my fault, the children in care it's all my fault." Before I can stop her she runs from the room. The hem of her skirt has come undone in the front and as she rushed down the corridor fumbling in her bag for a cigarette she hits her elbow in the door frame. Outside in the car park there is a man waiting for her - he stands huddled against the tree. The strong wind taking all the hair from his face making him look quite pinched.

Love from Karen

I go and visit Karen, she's nine years old. Her mother is an alcoholic, her father is unknown. Brother Francis is in care some miles away, she sees him every week. Karen is also in care and lives with foster parents. Her mother does not wish to visit her as she claims it will upset her and admits that 'in any case I feel guilty as hell and can't deal with it'.

Karen is waiting for me when I arrive. She is sitting tense and alone on the settee. I sit next to her. Usually she snuggles up to me but today she appears rigid and frightened. 'You tell your social worker what you've done' begins the foster mother. 'All of it?' she asks. 'All of it.' The child stares up and bites her lip. 'Promise nothing terrible will happen if I tell you,' she asks. I tell her that I promise. 'You see I was in a sweet shop and I stole some of these chews and a bar of honeycomb and chocolate for my brother. I did it with Mrs Simmonds' daughter, we got caught and the man from the sweet shop came here after us and now I think I have to leave here because I'm leading everyone astray.' As she tells me this she climbs onto my lap and throws her small arms around my neck. 'Also I put up two fingers at the teacher in class today and now I have to sit at the back of the class and I can't hear anything' she sobs. 'Also I can't use knives and forks properly because we don't have them at home, only spoons and I keep dropping them.' I talk with the foster mother and before I leave Karen runs upstairs and brings down several small items. 'This is for you, so you won't forget to visit me again.' It is a small photograph of herself taken at school. There is also a child's picture book which she tells me to give to her mother if I see her. 'Your mum will like that I'm sure,' I say as I leave. 'Make sure she reads it all,' adds Karen. In the car I thumb through the book and inside two letters drop out. They read:

- Dear Mummy, please will you visit me ever? I have been a very good girl. perhaps I shan't ever see you again. I have bought you some soap. Tomorrow is firework day. I love you Mummy. Come soon. Love from Karen.

I will say that

Joan talks about her marriage. "But I don't know really what happened. I went back and he started on saying how it was all my fault and that he'd had chances too and now he is going to do what I did, you know go off with someone else. But I'm never going back to him again and all those bills, they aren't mine I'm not paying them. He says he will strangle me, he will you know, he'll kill me. He doesn't want me now anyway. I don't know what will happen from one day to the next. He told me that he'd let me know when I could "phone him and we'd talk. Not that I'm going to be in when he rings. He put those plants in the garden last weekend and told me to go to the doctor about my rash, he can be a good man at times, I will say that. Down at the pub he told them a pack of lies about me, said I'd been carrying on and then I asked him who that woman was that rang up. No. I'm never going back to him but then he doesn't want me anyway. Oh I don't know I'm just so confused you've got to help me you must."

Ante natal ward

In the Day Room the girls talk together all day, flip through old magazines and baby catalogues and use the mobile telephone. The room is thick with smoke, they are all at various stages of pregnancy.

"I've been here for three months now, low Oestrogen level see, I lost the other baby at 6 months, that was a boy - I called him Dean after his dad. I get really bored here I just sit smoking and watching telly. They keep telling me about smoking but I got nothing else to do and I get worried."

She shifts her enormous frame from the low plastic chair, moves some stray bleached locks from across her face to behind her ear which has two single emerald stone earrings on each lobe. There is another hole punched but there is no earring in it. "My bleeding back aches I know that much," she says. "Men, what do they know about all this. My old man don't want me home, he's knocking off the girl next door. I reckon she's a single mother cause I've never seen the same man go in there and they all come out laughing. He's always fancied her anyway. He comes in here to see me once a week and brings me the bills and he stinks of booze."

"They're going to induce me tomorrow. I'm so scared. They use a pessary and the pains come on really quick. I saw a girl yesterday on this ward doubled up and her waters broke a few minutes after the pessary went in. I hope they 'phone my husband in time, sometimes it happens so quickly and he might miss it. He's looking forward to this baby, says he's going to call it Kevin whether it's a boy or not, after Kevin Keegan the footballer. I'm wondering if the baby is alright because they keep monitoring it and sometimes it feels funny. Yesterday they had a power cut in here and I was on the monitor and the sound of the baby's breathing stopped. I thought he was dead, it gave me a right shock."

"I got a friend who had a baby and she said that having it was that painful she almost died of a heart attack. Mind you she had a 9lb baby and 15 stitches. Her husband was there and he fainted, he had to be admitted onto the men's ward. Fat lot of good he was. My mate met someone who'd had a baby without any arms or legs and they wouldn't let her see the baby afterwards, my mate said it was because she drank a lot of vodka when she was first pregnant to try and get rid of it. I'm looking forward to having my baby, I hope it's a girl. What you had?" She turns round to ask me. I tell her. "Oh good, there's too many men about I'd say."

Labour ward

I am laying on my bed in the small room with my newly born daughter beside me. In the corridor outside the Ward Orderlies are stacking away piles of fresh clean linen into the cupboard. They are talking and laughing so loudly. "I couldn't watch them with another couple, I'd get too excited and have to ask them to go home. As it is my husband and I can't wait for the children to go to bed. That's why we're buying another video for the bedroom, then we can watch it with no one barging in. Really gets my husband going I can tell you, me too. The other night we had a real crude one called 'The Cat, The Man and The Curtain'. I never did figure out where the curtain fitted in but anyway she was holding this thing and the cat walks in and then I got called away but the children squabbling upstairs and so I missed it but when I came back they were cutting it up and eating it ...

"My old man and I sit there of a night waiting for the children to go to bed so we can get started watching it, we look at one another laughing. Saturday afternoon, like today, he'll go down to the Video Club and get some more. Hope he brings back the one of the big black man - he's like a bloody monkey!"

"Especially abroad you've got to forgive a lot haven't you? Our manager at the hotel was German, I know that's why the food was as bad. We had veal with tuna fish and tomato sauce in Spain, it was green and red. I like veal but not with fish, don't smell right somehow. My husband touched the waitress up at our table. I told him off but we got two helpings of chips. You don't realise how much weight you've put on until you put your skirt on to come home. I drank that much beer. I remember the night just before we came home we had fried kippers and a salad made from olives and brazil nuts and we had some purple Spanish liqueur. Me and Brian was throwing up all night."

"If she thinks I'm doing it she'll have a surprise. I'm sick of her leaving the side room for the day staff. That's the third time she'd left that note on the door. I tell you I'm pissing well cheesed off here, I am. She comes down here hoity-toity, Miss Marks and Spencers 1979, she thinks she can boss us all up. Well, I'm going to see Mr York today and tell him he can stuff his job up his arse or he can tell her to stuff her arse out the door."

Post natal

By the beds of all the women is a tiny plastic cot on wheels. Delighted parents and relatives peer inside or cuddle the baby. The new mothers are excited, bleary, tearful and tired. In the nursery where the staff teach you how to bath the baby and feed it we all gather by request, eager to learn how to cope with this new life.

"I haven't slept now for four days. I don't think I'll ever sleep again. I've had that many stitches I think the doctor must have been to embroidery classes. I can't sit down or stand up and I'm feeling faint all the time. I wish I had some energy to pick up the baby. I feel so dreadful." She begins to cry and we hand her a piece of green kitchen roll to dry her eyes on. "I've only seen my husband once since he was born and then I don't think he was very pleased, he can't cook for himself you see and his mother has gone on holiday." Her baby screams from its plastic cot and waves its minute arms in protest. "I can't breast feed it, I can't. I don't care what they say, I'm bottle feeding it. Why does it always cry like this? I don't think it likes me. Look at his little face all crumpled up like that, isn't he sweet?" She picks up the baby and holds him against her face making him quite wet with her tears.

"I don't know what I'm going to call her. I hadn't thought about any girls' names. I just wanted a boy really. Still she's a lovely baby alright but it's a pity she ain't a boy. I can't really call her Steve can I? That's after her dad. He was called Steve." I ask whether he is still called Steve. "Oh yeah, I expect so. I haven't seen him for about 2 months. Someone told me he'd gone to Folkestone to live with his dad so I don't know if I'll see him again."

"I knew there was something wrong with the baby when I was carrying her. They told me when I had the scan. They said so. She's a Mongol baby. They can't make me take it home you know. My husband wants to keep it but I can't, I just can't. They can't make me take it home you know. I haven't seen her since she was born. I had an anaesthetic anyway when she was born but I did see her the next day and she was ugly and all squinty eyed and squashed looking. They've given me tranquillisers. I want to go home. My husband's going round home with my mum today and they're going to take all the baby's clothes away. She's in the Special Care Unit now. They keep asking me if I want to go and see her. They can't make me take her home can they?"

A right laugh he is

Warren calls in to see me. He is eight years old and the youngest of three sons. His older brother Wayne is eleven and bald from the shaving of his head with an electric razor last week. The oldest Frank is known in and outside of the family as Wank. Wank, or should I say Frank, is due to go to Detention Centre for the second time this year. He thoughtlessly stole the front double gate from the home of a local magistrate and sold it later the same night to a local farmer around the corner for twenty pounds. Warren tells me all his news. He has had a good Christmas. Loads of toys and also saw his father just before the New Year. Quite an event since he hadn't actually seen him in four years and therefore had only vague and slight recollections of him built upon things overheard. "We have a new man living with us now though," he says as he walks towards the window and kicks at the wall. "He's called Ripper, a right laugh he is." "Why is he called Ripper?" I ask. "Oh I dunno. I suppose it is because he rips my mum's clothes off." Warren sits down on a chair; his feet don't touch the floor so he swings them continually. Now and again they hit the rung, hard, but he seems not to feel it. "Ripper looks after us. It's good really. My mum tells him not to have any rubbish from us lot but you know what Wank's like, he always spoils things. Mum says for him to smack Wank in the mouth if he won't do as he's asked. The other night he kicked him up the stairs when he wouldn't go to bed." "What did Frank say to that?" I ask. "Oh nothing really, he just sort of stayed in bed and when he got up in the morning all the pillow was red with blood from where Ripper has kicked him."

Seven pieces from the sauna

I

"Life without men is such a relief" she said. "Their strong hands and hair curling across warm shoulders. You can do without it," she said. "All that dressing up and the looking and the waiting and the hopes. What a relief," she said, "to be without hope."

II

"Luck. I was born lucky. Totally devoid of it," she said. She laughed. "At the nurseries today a coachload of young bronzed Dutchmen came to look around the tomato house and all the girls came out and flirted. A whole coachload of men and who do I get - the female teacher comes and talks to me. Luck, I was born without luck, totally devoid of it." She laughs.

III

"Oh the effort to be healthy," she said as she sweated away her huge limbs on the wooden slats. "Ten years I've worked on that Hoffman Press. For ten years that metal bar has struck into my side. Look, look," she said and showed me the dent and mark where the machine had injured her. "That's why my legs are so huge," she said. "You can't stand for ten years and not expect a result can you?"

IV

I told the Judge I did when I came to the Court. I don't want no maintenance from him. He can keep his money and his smell. But you can't reason with men can you and he made me take £4 for the girl but of course he never paid so we had to go back to Court and I told the Judge then I said 'his money stinks worst than what he does and I don't want it and he don't want to give it.' 'You're a special sort of woman' the Judge said and it made me feel all sort of glowing and happy just to see an important man like that say those things to me."

V

"They measure your legs and then they wrap you up in these bandages, tight as you can stand, then they cover it with cold stuff like unset jelly and then they leave you. We didn't half laugh me mate and I. Then they take it off and measure you again and let you hold the tape measure so as there can be no cheating and you can see what you've lost. It's great. I lost three inches off my hips and two off my thighs. I don't know where the fat goes, they say it distributes it. All I know is that mine was all back by the end of the week."

VI

"He was conceived because I got an electric shock. I was plugging in the washing machine, I had wet hands and the next thing I knew I was on the floor on the other side of the room with my arm and hand all black and the nails gone and the arm jerking up and down. I was in a right state I can tell you. I rang me mum and we went to the hospital. I was in for two nights. Well I never took the pill those two nights did I and when I got home we conceived him. I didn't give it any thought. But he died at eighteen months old. Hole on the heart. I'm not being horrible or nothing but it was best really, seeing how the marriage was all wrong. I took him to the hospital almost every day at one time but he still died. Bill left the day after he died. He never even came to the funeral. He used to smoke Players and the morning of the funeral he put a note through the door written on the back on an old Players packet saying:

'Can't come. I am working.'

Just that on the Players packet. Not even Dear Sandra or Love Bill. I didn't cry about him dying for three months. I had Theresa to look after see and I was all alone, so alone and then one day I lost my purse which was the end of the world for me as I had no money at all. I ran into my neighbour and she put her arms around me and said "Never mind love it's only a purse with a few bob in it." I cried and cried and cried. No-one had touched me you see for such a long time and I suddenly let it all go. I never have cried in front of my mum. I like her, I feel sorry for her actually but she can't accept me when I'm weak. I always have to be strong for her otherwise she'll just say again 'you should never have let Bill leave you like that, you have to work at marriage you know."

VII

"Do you live in town?" the woman with short dark hair wearing only her locket asks me. "No, no," I tell her, "I live out across the marsh." She shifts uneasily on the warm slate. "How about you, you local?" I ask. "Yes we live over Stanhope Estate. You know it?" I tell her I know it. "I can't stay in here long as I'd like to today as my old man will be waiting outside. He's changed his shift this week as he reckons I'm up to something while he's at work, thought he'd catch me out today he did by changing shift without mentioning it first. Slimy bugger he is. I've got nothing to hide, more's the pity I'd say. I work at the Fish Restaurant in town. I used to think it was a right hovel 'till I went to work there meself. Often my old man would say to me on a Friday night, 'Take you out to the Fish Restaurant, save you cooking,' and I'd say 'Last of the big spenders, no jolly fear, I might catch me death what with it being fish as well. But it's not that bad, in fact I'm seeing if I can work longer hours just in case I need to." "Need to?" I ask. "I might be leaving my old man soon you see and I'm going to want the money. The solicitor says I've got more than enough grounds so I'm thinking about it. We've been that unhappy for years now and it's only a matter of time. He's had so many girlfriends, they still 'phone him up and I answer and I say to them - 'Lover boy's at St Moritz I'm afraid,' then I hang up. He's not at all exciting to look at, so I can't understand it. Most people wouldn't want to look once at him, let alone twice, but there's no accounting for taste is there? Take me for example, and I wish someone would. I used to think he was great at one time, five years ago. Now? Now I just think he's a barrel of shit." She shifts her hot red body on the wooden slats. "Cor my bum's hot," she says. "What about you, you married? Don't answer that I can guess - you look too well to be married. Well, it's all over now and that's for sure. One night we had just finished dinner at home, lovely dinner I'd cooked - pork chops, carrots, roast potatoes, peas. I can see it now. But anyway I'd had a very curious day with him not talking and me keeping out of sight just talking to the cat but anyway I still made dinner, lovely dinner and he ate it and read the paper, fell asleep. Sometimes I was relieved when he fell asleep because at least I didn't have to try and avoid him did I? But I was buggered if I was going to wash up and clear away after all the trouble I'd taken. So he fell asleep and I read me book and the next day they were still there and the next and the next too.

"They just sat there for a week and a half going mouldy. They went bright green in the end. They became a sort of monument if you know what I mean, a monument to our marriage. It all represented his lack of feeling for us and my dislike of him. Being pork of course it solidified and caked up and went a very strange kind of white and purple mixed in with the green.

"Eventually I threw it all out, plates, cutlery and all. 'I don't know why you did that,' he said as I closed the dustbin lid on it all. 'Don't you,' I said, 'Don't you even trouble your head wondering about it then.' I was that upset. So you see it'd been a right loveless match from day one and I'm only too glad of this job at the Fish Restaurant so I can save up me money and buzz off." She moves her large limbs and makes to go. She fumbles at her neck touching the locket. "Cor that's got bloody hot sitting here" "Who gave it to you? It's pretty," I say. "Oh he did of course. He's always generous with his money and his bloody moods."

No life into him

I visit Grace. "Sit down, sit down," she says. "I've just been thinking, I've just been thinking about all those terrible days when the baby died and now I see his ghost all the time, you've got to make it go away."

Grace has been discharged from the mental hospital for just two days now and she sits sewing a grubby white dress which she tells me is to be her wedding dress when she marries another patient she met in hospital six months ago. He is still an in-patient and likely to remain so for some time. Her first marriage ended in divorce and he hasn't been seen in the eight years since. Years ago Grace had lived in an old caravan with the children outside of a small Kent village; they were not gypsies or travellers but they were the talk of the town. Grace has told me her story many times before and I sit on the moquet chair that's stuck together with dirt and impacted grease of years and Justin the Alsatian dog sniffs in my pocket.

"He hadn't been ill and was screaming so loud and Jim was shouting too and the two little ones were out shopping and Ben and Francis were working out the back chopping logs. So I picked him up and put him outside in the pram to give us all a bit of peace. Finally he stopped screaming and I went back into the caravan to peel the potatoes and start the tea. It was April and it didn't seem all that cold really. Anyway I called the boys in so they could have their tea before the little ones came back and then Jim and I had our tea. They came running in saying 'Mum, Mum, the baby's all blue and stiff, look, look!' I ran out and Jim ran out but we could get no life into him, he was dead. The doctor said the cold killed him but I just think he stopped living. He wasn't ever happy."

Grace then sobs for a long time and paces the room with the huge dog following her every movement. "And now I see him all the time, I sleep downstairs now as I'm too afraid to go upstairs but he comes up to where I lay on the sofa tugging at my nightdress calling 'Mummy, Mummy let me in I'm cold'."

Tommy

Tommy is a chatty and open child. He has four sisters who call him 'champ'.
He has a photograph of his father but he doesn't look at it very often.
When he was born his father left the family. 'I don't like boys,' he told his daughters and wife. 'I don't like Tommy.'
Two weeks later he set up home three blocks away with a woman who had two boys.
Tommy never knew his father but once he saw him collecting the boys from the school gate. Arm in arm they were.
When he was six years old his father bought him a five foot teddy and Tommy calls it 'Big Dad'.
It's very soft and warm and Tommy keeps his clothes on it at night.

Lee

"Yes I did shout out 'Shut up you little cunt' to the baby but I didn't hit him."
"She was running down the stairs with the baby and his head was shaking side to side - it must have been the shaking what caused the injury."
"She shouldn't have sold my radio then I wouldn't have been so angry but that kid cried all of the time anyway."
"The neighbours heard it, banged on the walls at us. She never had any patience with the kid. She threw her boots at him when he cried at night."
He stubs his roll-up onto the bare floor.
"So what if I did shout out 'Shut up you little cunt,' at the baby? He deserved it crying all the time, he should have learnt by now; he's six months old."

Wendy

The child was tiny for her age, short, thin, odd.
A lack of love since birth, constant separations from a mother who once blinded her sister in a rage.
The child disliked food and lacked any ability to show enthusiasm.
Those who know call it emotional dwarfism.
Constantly wary and on guard she hears the conversation of adults three rooms away. An unpopular child with controlling manner and sinister gaze. The five year old greets me slowly. She draws minute figures for me and tells of her dreams in which a 'huge witch will come and take me away from here gobbling me up as she flies'.

Mark

He was locked into a room with his four brothers and two sisters for three days before the police broke in.
Finding his mother collapsed and hysterical in the kitchen demented from the pressures of her solitary and luckless life, the policewoman removed the potato peeler from her limp white hands before escorting her into the ambulance. The children were hungry but not unhappy. The baby had slept for twenty hours after crying for fifteen. One of the older ones had painted the walls with excreta.
Mark can remember some of it but hasn't seen his mother since the day she closed the door. He is curious about his brothers and misses his baby sister.
Mark is waiting for a new family to adopt him. He writes stories about a hunch-backed boy who lived in a cave and he always asks me if I will love him forever.

He left us

Dawn is a difficult girl, her mother is afraid of her tempers. They remind her of her own. Her father left them three years ago for a woman half his age with a car, energy and no demands.

I am asked to talk some sense into Dawn. I ask her what music she likes. "I don't know," she says. I ask if she has a boyfriend. "I don't know," she says. "People at school are worried about you, your mum is concerned that you are so depressed," I say. "I don't care," she says. In the corner her mother sits and weeps and I suggest she leaves us alone. She does. "Your mother is depressed and tired," I say. "I hate her," she replies. "She's so miserable and weak and let my dad go off with that woman. I hate him too, he left us, he left me." Dawn's large angular body is laying on the settee, her acned face is streaked with her old make-up. "Was it all her fault?" I ask. "I don't know," she says. Her mother comes back into the room and the two women look at one another for a second before looking away again.

Odd but deeper

Robert says "See I just woke up some time last month and asked one of the staff what the time was and my throat felt all sort of odd, not sore exactly but strained. I thought it was probably all that glue sniffing that I'd done but then when I shouted at me mate across the football pitch it seemed to make a queer sound and not come out really". We walk together through the grounds of the children's home where Robert lives now and he shows me some new bulbs appearing through the soil around the base of the trees. "That reminds me," he says, "I must have been here nearly a year now because the flowers were all out the day you brought me here. Anyway as I was saying I shouted across the football pitch and nothing came out but then eventually it did and it sounded odd but deeper. For a few days I hardly spoke to anyone because they rib you something rotten here. Then me mum 'phoned me up and she said 'Who's that?' and I said, 'It's me, Robert,' and she said 'Get off it ain't'. I said 'It is, it is me'. Then she said 'Your voice has broken,' and I said 'Yes I know'." We walk back to the house and I tell Robert how he is taller than me now and he laughs and says "That's not very hard, is it?"

Too slow you see

"She was one of the last ones out when it came to it. The last one out of the dug-out. She was too slow you see and in any case they didn't care that much where she was at any given time. I always did though. She'll always be my baby, my June."

She hugs the fifty year old Downs Syndrome woman to her breast. "When she was five they didn't believe in them going to school, they wanted me to send her away. You'll get tired of it, they said. I said I wouldn't and I didn't and I haven't, much as they know or care. I will always remember her being the last one out of the dug-out after the bomb fell. Her little face bewildered and lost. It made her afraid of being alone for life."

June looks up. Tells me she wants to make me a Calendar. She makes them all year round for the year just past.

In sickness and in health

Mrs James is tired and worn after the weekend. Her husband tried to commit suicide again and she is left to calm the children down. Mr James went out on Sunday night to a local quiet spot, drilled a hole through the floor of their maroon Cortina, placed a hose through the floor to the exhaust pipe, put the other end under a woollen blanket then sat underneath it and breathed in deeply. He was there for some hours; his jacket had caught over the hole and he had eventually woken quite dazed and driven home. Mrs James had been searching for him, so had the neighbours and the police. She brought the blanket and green plastic hose pipe to show me. They were burnt black and stank of carbon monoxide. Mrs James leant against me and she cried. "Tell me," she said, "Tell me why I love him, all the terrible things he's done to me over the years, the injuries, the bruising. I've seen the police doctor before when he's clouted me so hard. But he's always been the same, never know when he will change, for years he's been moody. One day you think your life is in order, you relax and then snap, off he goes again. I'm just terrified of him now, a permanent state of fear. The children just avoid him. The other night I came home from work, cooked the tea, cleared up, did the washing, sat down asked what was on TV. Well he went berserk, threw his book at me, shouted that I was a lazy cow. How do you have respect for a man like that? Now of course he's had this breakdown and I have to chase all over for him and hide his pills and put up with it. He's so pathetic really I could cry for him if I wasn't so afraid of him. In sickness and in health, my God in sickness ..." We stare at the blanket and the green hose lying on the floor.

Chances

Billy is serving a life sentence in a Kent prison. He is twenty-two years old. At eighteen he and two other men went into an off licence with two sawn-off shotguns and demanded the takings. The manager declined and they shot him at point blank range in the chest. Dead. They ran outside and into the police van.

At the Assizes the Judge summed up by saying that Billy had been given every chance in the past to be an honest citizen but that he clearly had now shown that he was unable to be trusted. In view of the cold blooded murder of the Ruislip manager of the Off Licence Billy would go to prison for life. He tells me about it. "I was numb man, totally numb. I knew I'd go down for a long time but I didn't think it would be forever. I was just lost when I was eighteen. I'm more lost now. They say I might get out in another twelve years if I'm good. I used to work in the tyre factory but I was black and I had no woman. I wanted money. Fast. I suppose I was given every opportunity. I came into care when I was seven years old. My mum disappeared you see and they put me in one of those homes where some nice women cared for me. My sister was in care too but I never saw her, she was three miles away in another home. I went to a good school, we had a uniform. I was good at school but I could have done better. I had a grey blazer with a badge. At fifteen I was still in care and I had this social worker who let me meet my sister. She'd grown a bit in those eight years, she looked like a whippet without legs. I liked the social worker, he was a good bloke, gave me fags - you got any? Well anyway I then started taking things from a shop and then I didn't go to school and I kicked a bloke's head in at the home. After that it all seemed to happen. I got caught stealing again and then I went to Detention Centre for six months. I got really fit that six months. Muscles like barrels. I had met some good mates. I came out and I used to fold up my blankets and do hospital corners. The home couldn't believe it. Anyway then I had to leave the home as they was closing down so I went into a hostel. I started work at the tyre factory and then out of the blue after ten years my mum came to see me. She arrived on my doorstep at the hostel with a new geezer who tried to push me around. One night he got really heavy so I showed him. I broke his jaw. Anyway I did go and live with my mum again and then I met this girl, really nice girl she was, we got on well but then one night we had a fight and I split her lip. She'd been good to me she had. Yes, well then I met these blokes in a pub one night and finally we got together this plan for the Off Licence. We worked it out, took over six months. We didn't intend to kill anyone you know. It just happened. Johnny got these shooters from his brother. I had never used one before.

"The Judge was right though I did have opportunities in my life didn't I? I suppose I just didn't take them.

"I work in the kitchens now here. I start at 6am and finish at 7pm. It kills the time. I earn good money and can buy me records. It scares me shitless to think of going out of here. It's all I think about, getting out and what I'll do. But it does terrify me. I don't think I'll cope. I just want a good woman to settle down with. Still I try not to think about it. When you've got a life sentence tomorrow's a long way off.

"Funny really talking about all this, my old lady came to see me yesterday and she said it was all my dad's fault for kicking her around because then she wouldn't have gone off and left us. But I don't know. I reckon it was the best thing she ever did."

Right at the peak of season

Deal is flooded, several feet under water in parts. Homes ruined, people uprooted from their homes. A tragedy. A declared disaster area. A handicapped woman living close to the sea wall has been pinned into her home by shale, drifting wood and rubble. The army and police force her door open and let me in. Luckily the house has escaped much water damage but there is no gas or electricity and for thirty hours she has sat cold and terrified. I ask her if she would like to move out for a while but she refuses telling me how, until seven years ago she had worked as a lavatory attendant on the front here at Deal. "For years watching the women come and go and some of the things I've seen my dear." She begins to cry. "I'm sorry it's just being trapped here for so long and being unable to move and the dark and no heat." We are told that gas and electricity will be restored shortly and until then she speaks to me of her working life on the front and her fun and laughter with the man from 'the Gents' and how he died on the job one summer morning right at the peak of the season.

Up town for a bit

Julia has come into the office to see me. She comes in every week on a Wednesday at 2.30 by order of the Court. She is supposed to come after school but we both know that she hasn't been for a month but at sixteen years old, a diagnosed mental age of twelve and three weeks before leaving day there doesn't seem much point. Julia's parents are divorcing, her sister is due in Court for stabbing an animal to death and there are important things on her mind other than school.

She stands in the doorway, a large girl wearing a padded jacket underneath her padded anorak, it makes her seem enormous. Julia has shaved her head in the week which makes her face seem even larger and her spots bigger. "Do you like me hair?" she asks. "I'm going to get a job shelf filling at the precinct and I thought this seemed genic." I ask if she would like to sit down. "No, I can't stop, Brian's outside waiting and we're going up town for a bit." I ask how her mum and dad are getting on "Oh them, they're like a couple of Tom cats. Anyway I got to go now. I'm glad you like me hair."

Julia slams the door after her and I watch her disappear across the car park alone. There is no Brian and there is no shelf filling job. Just an oversized young woman with her shaved head and a sadness.

It's this house

Mrs White is a large woman. I sit on her PVC sofa while we talk about her child who, at eighteen months old, she claims, is maladjusted and violent like his older brother. Mrs White tells me that the child doesn't respond to discipline of any kind and throws his toys at her. He had cried solidly almost for two whole months after he was born; nothing would pacify him. His birth had been difficult and it was some time before Mrs White was able to cuddle him. She had been told that he may die as he seemed unable to digest his food although there were no discovered medical reasons. Mrs White has her theories. The child was one of a twin, the other being born dead, the body had begun to decompose; she was sure it was a punishment. An Indian doctor had told her at the ante-natal clinic that the twins were well and thriving and that in his opinion all twins were in communication in utereo. Mrs White was certain the baby was in mourning for his twin and that the trauma of it made him cry non-stop. Mr White sits in the corner of the room quietly while we talk; he watches half smiling. He begins to speak and so does Mrs White. He interjects loudly "Be quiet woman. You stupid cow". He glares at her. "Let me speak you ignorant bitch." I look at him waiting for his words. "Bloody child cries all the time, it's violent too, you should do something about it, you people, you should do your jobs better, call yourself social workers!" Before I can ask him what he feels should be done he gets up and storms out of the room and we hear him mumbling as he walks up the stairs. "Bloody bitch, bloody bitch." Mrs White and I remain on the PVC sofa; she is in tears. "It's this house," she says, "It's this house..."

Books by Elaine Randell

Songs of Hesperus	Curiously Strong Press, 1972
Telegrams From the Midnight Country	Blacksuede Boot Press, 1973
Untitled	Sceptre Press, 1973
Seven Poems	Transgravity Press, 1973
A Taper to the Outward Roome	Laundering Room Press, 1974
Long Hair for Birds	Joe Dimaggio Press, 1974
Early in My Life	Permanent Press, 1977
Larger Breath of All Things	Spectacular Diseases, 1978
This, Our Frailty	Oasis Books, 1979
Songs for the Sleepless	Pig Press, 1982
Beyond All Other	Pig Press, 1986
Gut Reaction	North and South, 1987

Elaine Randell was born in September 1951, at Charing Cross Hospital, London. Her early life was spent in South London. In the 1960s she began AMAZING GRACE magazine and worked in many fields including rare books, antique silver and journalism.

Elaine qualified as a social worker and art therapist in the 1970s and has been a child care and mental health practitioner for Social Services Departments in London and Kent. Most recently she has worked for the Church of England Children's Society in the adoption of older and handicapped children. She now works as a Guardian and ad litem in local courts.

Elaine Randell is married with three daughters; Phoebe aged four years, Beatrice aged two years and Naomi just born. She lives in the heart of the Kent countryside with her husband Ian, Soay sheep, chickens, geese and two English setter dogs.